Lemon-Almond Crusted Cod

Serves: 4

Preparation Time: 50 minutes

Ingredients

- Onions (600g
- Vegetable stock (1 tablespoon, unsalted)
- Balsamic vinegar (130ml)
- Almonds (70g, chopped)
- Olive oil (2 teaspoons)
- Codfish (450g
- Water (65ml)
- Spinach (1kg)
- Olive oil (1 ½ teaspoons)
- Orange juice (130ml, freshly squeezed)
- Lemon zest (from 1 lemon)
- Dill (1 tablespoon, fresh)
- Pepper
- Dijon mustard (4 teaspoons)
- Garlic (6 cloves, chopped)
- Lemon juice (freshly squeezed)

Directions

- Heat a pot of water and add onions; leave in water for 15 seconds then drain and add cold water to onions and drain again. Remove peels from onion and roots.

- Heat stock and oil in a skillet and add onions; cook for 6 minutes until golden spots appear. Put in vinegar and orange juice and heat until it boils. Lower heat, stirring and scraping bits from pot; cook for 10 minutes until tender (use a knife to test onion). Take onions from pot and put into a bowl and continue to boil for 3 minutes until mixture is syrupy. Pour sauce on top of onion and cover to keep warm.

- Set oven to 400°F/200°C and use cooking spray or oil to coat a baking sheet. Mix together zest, dill, pepper, almonds and 2 teaspoons oil. Use 1 teaspoon mustard to spread onto each piece of fish then press into almond blend.

- Bake for 9 minutes while heating stock in a pot. Put in lemon juice, pepper and cook for 4 minutes. Add garlic, stir and cook for 2 minutes.

- Serve spinach along with fish.

Nutritional Info

Calories 371.5
Carbs 38g
Fat 12g
Protein 31g

Pecan Baked Tilapia

Serves: 4

Preparation Time: 35 minutes

Ingredients

- Panko breadcrumbs (30g)
- Brown sugar (1/2 teaspoon)
- Cayenne pepper
- Egg white (1)
- Raw pecans (40g, chopped)
- Rosemary (2 teaspoons, chopped)
- Olive oil (1 ½ teaspoons)
- Tilapia (4 filets)

Directions

- Set oven to 350°F/180°C.

- Combine pecans, sugar, cayenne pepper and breadcrumbs together in a baking dish. Put in oil and mixture to coat.

- Bake mixture for 8 minutes until golden.

- Adjust oven temperature to 400°F/200°C. Use cooking spray or oil to coat a baking dish and whisk egg white in a small dish. Coat filets one at a time with egg white and then with pecan mixture.

- Place into greased baking dish and top with any leftover pecan mixture.

- Bake for 10 minutes.

- Serve.

Nutritional Info

Calories 206.5
Carbs 5.3g
Fat 10.1g
Protein 24.8g

Salmon with Baby Arugula

Serves: 2

Preparation Time: 25 minutes

Ingredients

- Salmon (2 center cut filets)
- Olive oil (1 ½ tablespoons)
- Black pepper
- Lemon juice (1 ½ tablespoons)
- All purpose seasoning (1/8 teaspoon)

- **For salad:**

- Cherry tomatoes (130g, cut in half)
- Black pepper
- Wine vinegar (1 tablespoon)
- Baby arugula (60g)
- Red onion (40g, sliced)
- Olive oil (1 tablespoon, extra virgin)

Directions

- Season fish with all purpose, oil and lemon juice; marinate for 15 minutes.

- Heat skillet and place the salmon onto the skin side into the pot and cook for 3 minutes. Use a spatula to lightly lift fish to avoid sticking.

- Lower heat and cover pan; cook for 4 minutes until skin is crispy.

- Combine onion, tomatoes and arugula in a bowl then drizzle with vinegar and oil.

- Serve salad with fish.

Nutritional Info

Calories 390
Carbs 4g
Fat 23g
Protein 40g

Baked Cod & Green Beans

Serves: 1

Preparation Time: 30 minutes

Ingredients

- Olive oil (2 teaspoons)
- Cod (120g)
- Green beans (300g)
- Blueberries (50g)
- Old-fashioned oats (1 tablespoon)
- Tomato (2 slices)

Directions

- Set oven to 400°F/200°C.
- Combine oats and half of oil in a bowl and use mixture to coat fish.
- Coat baking tray with cooking spray and place fish onto tray and top with the tomato slices and bake for 15 minutes.
- Steam green beans and serve with fish and blueberries.

Nutritional Info

Calories 350
Carbs 39g
Fat 11g
Protein 27g

Baked Scallops

Serves: 1

Preparation Time: 30 minutes

Ingredients

- Bay scallops (90g)
- Oats (1 tablespoon, old-fashioned)
- Olive oil (1 ½ teaspoons, extra-virgin)
- Lemon pepper
- Garbanzo beans (50g, low salt)
- Cucumber (150g)
- White wine (3 tablespoons)
- Cheddar cheese (15g, low fat, shredded)
- Lemon juice (3 tablespoons, freshly squeezed)
- Romaine lettuce (230g, chopped)
- Tomato (1)

Directions

- Put scallops into a container and cover with white wine; cover container and put into refrigerator overnight.

- Set oven to 350°F/180°C.

- Remove scallops from wine and top with oats and cheese.

- Place onto a baking tray and bake for 10 minutes.

- Combine lemon pepper, lemon juice and oil in a small bowl.

- Mix together garbanzo beans, cucumber, lettuce and tomato.

- Serve salad topped with lemon dressing and baked scallops.

Nutritional Info

Calories 358
Carbs 34g
Fat 11g
Protein 27g

Orzo and Spiced Shrimp

Serves: 2

Preparation Time: 40 minutes

Ingredients

- Orzo pasta (150g)
- Olive oil (1 tablespoon)
- Black pepper
- Chile powder (1/2 teaspoon, ancho)
- Cumin (1/4 teaspoon)
- Cayenne pepper
- Lime juice (3 tablespoons, freshly squeezed)
- Red onion (1/2, sliced)
- Basil leaves (2 tablespoons)
- Smoked paprika (1 teaspoon)
- Agave nectar (1 teaspoon)
- Coriander (1/4 teaspoon)
- Jumbo shrimp (90g, deveined and without shell)
- Lettuce (8 leaves)
- Tomatoes (2, sliced)

Directions

- Put oil and basil into a processor or blender and pulse until smooth. Add black pepper and lime juice, mx together and put aside until needed.

- Heat grill.

- Combine chili powder, cumin, cayenne pepper, paprika, sugar and coriander in a small bowl.

- Coat shrimp with cooking spray and spice blend and put aside; prepare orzo as directed on package, run under cold water and drain.

- Pour lime juice over orzo.

- Grill shrimp for 4 minutes until slightly charred.

- Place lettuce on a place and top with orzo, onion and tomato and drizzle with basil blend.

- Add shrimp and serve.

Nutritional Info

Calories 345
Carbs 35g
Fat 11g
Protein 26g

Apple Scallops

Serves: 1

Preparation Time: 15 minutes

Ingredients

- Celery (75g, diced)
- Vegetable broth (130ml, no salt)
- Ginger (1/2 teaspoon, grated)
- Cardamom (1 teaspoon)
- Olive oil (1 teaspoon)
- Carrot (15g, shredded)
- Green beans (1 cup)
- Green apple (3/4, without core and chopped)
- Scallops (120g)
- Walnuts (1 tablespoon, crushed)

Directions

- Add carrots and celery to pot along with 3 tablespoon broth and cook for 5 minutes.

- Put in leftover broth along with ginger, cardamom, green beans and apple; mix together to combine and cook until thoroughly heated.

- Heat skillet and coat with cooking spray and cook scallops on all sides until golden.

- Serve with vegetables and top with walnuts and olive oil.

Nutritional Info

Calories 324
Carbs 36g
Fat 11g
Protein 23g

Cajun Salmon

Serves: 1

Preparation Time: 30 minutes

Ingredients

- Bell pepper (90g, sliced)
- Salmon (140g)
- Broccoli (350g, chopped)
- Onion (40g, sliced)
- Cajun seasoning (1 teaspoon)
- Olive oil (1 teaspoon, extra-virgin)

Directions

- Set oven to 350°F/180°C. Use foil to line a baking sheet and coat with cooking spray or oil.

- Coat onions and pepper with cooking spray and put onto prepare baking sheet. Coat salmon with Cajun seasoning and put onto sheet long with broccoli.

- Bake for 25 minutes until fish is flaky.

- Serve fish accompanied by vegetables; drizzle oil over vegetables if so desired.

Nutritional Info

Calories 353
Carbs 40g
Fat 12g
Protein 26g

Shrimp and Chickpeas

Serves: 2

Preparation Time: 20 minutes plus chilling time

Ingredients

- Olive oil (1 tablespoon)
- Jalapeno (1, diced without seeds)
- Garlic (1 clove, diced)
- Lime juice (3 tablespoons, freshly squeezed)
- Canned garbanzo beans (100g, drained)
- Shrimp (210g, cooked)
- Chipotle (2 tablespoons, in adobo sauce, chopped)
- Red onion (150g, chopped)
- Tomato (600g, chopped)
- Cilantro (15g, chopped)

Directions

- Put chipotle, red onion, garlic, olive oil and jalapeno in a bowl; whisk together until thoroughly combined.

- Add lime juice, beans, tomato and cilantro to mixture and toss to combine.

- Adjust seasonings to desired taste and chill for at least 2 hours.

- Serve topped with shrimp.

Nutritional Info

Calories 357
Carbs 38g
Fat 11g
Protein 28g

Sea Bass and Carrots

Ingredients:

- 1 Large Courgette
- 1 Large Carrot – Peeled
- 1 tsp. of Coconut Oil
- Dash of Chili Flakes
- 2-4 Sea Bass Fillets
- Coriander – Chopped, Garnish

Directions:

- Spiral your courgette and the carrot.
- In a heavy pan, heat the coconut oil until it is hot.
- Add in the chili flakes and the sea bass. Put it in skin side down.
- After 3 minutes, turn the fillets over and cook it for another 3 minutes. Remove it and put it on a plate.
- Add in the courgette and the carrots. Stir-fry it for 2 minutes.
- Remove it from the heat and put it on the plates with the fish on top.
- Sprinkle the coriander on the top before you serve it.

Nutritional Information:

Calories: 175

Total Fat: 4g

Saturated Fat: 2g

Carbohydrates: 3g

Protein: 24g

Squid with Brown Rice Pasta

Ingredients:

- 510g of Brown Rice Pasta

- 60ml of Coconut Oil

- 510g of Squid – Rings

- 150g of Red Onion – Sliced Thin

- ½ tsp. of Crushed Chilies

- 2 Cloves of Garlic – Chopped Fine

- 1 Tbsp. of Sherry Vinegar

- Parsley – Chopped

Directions:

- Cook the pasta using the instructions on the package.

- Melt the coconut oil in a large pan.

- Sauté the onions and then add in the garlic. Cook it for 2-3 minutes. Stir it so that the onions and the garlic are completely mixed together.

- Add in the squid and the chilies. Cook it for 3-5 minutes. Make sure not to overcook it.

- Add in the sherry vinegar and the parsley. Stir it well.

Nutritional Information:

Calories: 246

Total Fat: 2g

Saturated Fat: 0g

Carbohydrates: 45g

Protein: 9g

Coconut Shrimp and Spicy Peach Dip

Ingredients:

- 2 Eggs

- 30g of Coconut Flour

- ¼ tsp. of Cayenne Pepper

- ¼ tsp. of Salt

- ¼ tsp. of Paprika

- 45g of Panko Breadcrumbs

- 30g of Shredded Coconut

- 500g of Shrimp – Deveined, Tails On

- 3 tbsp. Coconut Oil

Directions:

- Add in the eggs to a medium sized mixing bowl and whisk them together. Set it aside.

- Add in the coconut flour, salt, paprika, and the cayenne pepper. Set it aside.

- Add in the crumbs and the shredded coconut to a medium sized bowl. Put it aside.

- Pick the shrimp up by the tail and dip them in the flour mix.

- Dip them in the egg bowl, drip the egg-drenched shrimp in the coconut mix. Make sure it is coated well.

- Repeat the process until all of your shrimp are covered.

- Add 3 Tbsp. of coconut oil in a medium sized pan. Allow it to heat up for 3 minutes on medium low heat.

- Transfer the shrimp to the pan, working in batches. Cook them for 2 minutes on each side.

- Move the shrimp to a plate that is lined with a paper towel.

Nutritional Information:

Calories: 440

Total Fat: 16g

Saturated Fat: 7g

Carbohydrates: 20g

Protein: 53g

Spaghetti Squash and Shrimp Pesto

Ingredients:

- 1 Spaghetti Squash

- 500g of Shrimp – Peeled, Deveined

- 1 Tbsp. of Coconut Oil

- Dash of Salt

- Dash of Pepper

- Pesto

Directions:

- Slice the squash in half, lengthwise.

- Chop the ends off. Put both of the halves face down.

- Put an inch of water in the pan.

- Microwave it for 15 minutes (medium settings).

- Turn the dish at the halfway mark. It is done when the fork can easily go through the skin.

- Heat a medium sized pan with the oil. Wash and dry the shrimp thoroughly.

- Season it with pepper and salt.

- Add it to the pan and cook the shrimp on each side for 3-5 minutes.

- Once the squash is cooled down a bit, take a fork and run it through the inside to make strands.

- Continue it until you hit the skin.

- Put the squash in a bowl; top it with shrimp and the pesto.

Nutritional Information:

Calories: 260

Total Fat: 9g

Saturated Fat: 3g

Carbohydrates: 27g

Protein: 26g

Honey Balsamic Salmon

Ingredients:

- 2 Salmon Fillets
- ½ Tbsp. of Coconut Oil
- ½ Tbsp. of Honey
- 3 Tbsp. of Balsamic Vinegar
- 1 tsp. of Red Pepper Flakes
- Sea Salt
- Pepper

Directions:

- Heat the oil in a large pan on medium to high heat.
- Season both sides of the salmon with the salt and the pepper.
- Add the salmon to the pan and cook it 1-2 minutes on each side until it is brown.
- Whisk the honey, red pepper flakes, and vinegar in a small mixing bowl.
- Add the vinegar mix to the pan and simmer it until the fish is tender. It will take about 5 minutes.
- Reduce it to a simmer for 5-10 minutes.

Nutritional Information:

Calories: 300

Total Fat: 18g

Saturated Fat: 6g

Carbohydrates: 9g

Protein: 23g

Tilapia and Coconut Almonds

Ingredients:

- 500g of Tilapia Fillets
- 3.5g of Almonds – Unsalted
- 20g of Dried Coconut Flakes – Unsweetened
- Dash of Salt
- Dash of Pepper
- 1 Spray of Olive Oil or 4 tbsp. Oil
- Parsley
- Garlic Salt

Directions:

- Pre-heat your oven to 375°F/190°.

- Line your baking sheet with liner or parchment paper.

- Combine the coconut, almonds, parsley pepper, and salt.

- Pulse it in a food processor until it is combined well. It should feel like breadcrumbs.

- Lay your tilapia on the baking sheet.

- Sprinkle it with garlic salt.

- Sprinkle the coconut mix on the top of each piece of fish.

- Spray the fish with olive oil.

- Bake it for 20 minutes until it is browned and flakey.

Nutritional Information:

Calories: 424

Total Fat: 22g

Saturated Fat: 17g

Carbohydrates: 10g

Protein: 49g

Teriyaki Salmon

Ingredients:

- 2 Salmon Fillets
- 2 Tbsp. of Coconut Aminos
- 1 Tbsp. of Brown Sugar
- 1 Lemon
- 1 Tbsp. of Extra Virgin Olive Oil
- 1 Tbsp. of Ginger – Finely Chopped

Directions:

- Mix all of the ingredients together, except for the salmon.
- Put the fillets into an oven dish and cover it with the marinade.
- Spoon it over the fish a few times. Cover it with foil.
- Bake it for 20 minutes on 355°F/180°C.

Nutritional Information:

Calories: 160

Total Fat: 11g

Saturated Fat: 2g

Carbohydrates: 5g

Protein: 12g

Lime Coconut Shrimp

Ingredients:

- 3 Limes
- 1kg of Shrimp – Peeled, Deveined
- 420ml of Coconut Milk
- 1 Tbsp. of Salt
- ½ tsp. of Pepper
- 25g of Coconut Flakes

Directions:

- Use a greater to zest the limes and then set them aside.
- Squeeze two limes and then combine the juice with the coconut milk and your shrimp. Refrigerate it for 15-30 minutes.
- In the food processor, combine the lime zest, pepper, and the salt. Pulse it to blend it.
- Remove your shrimp from the marinade and put them in

Nutritional Information:

Calories: 206

Total Fat: 10g

Saturated Fat: 2g

Carbohydrates: 10g

Protein: 18g

Coconut Shrimp with Sweet and Sour Sauce

Ingredients:

- 55g of Flour
- ½ tsp. of Baking Powder
- ½ tsp. of Paprika
- ½ tsp. of Seasoned Salt
- 160ml of Water
- 45g of Bread Crumbs
- 120g of Shredded Coconut
- 500g of Shrimp – Deveined, Peeled

Sauce

- 600g of Pineapples Chunks with the Juice
- 3 Cloves of Garlic – Peeled
- 2 Tbsp. of Soy Sauce
- 2 Tbsp. of Corn Starch
- 1 Jalapeno Pepper
- 1 Red Bell Pepper
- 2 Tbsp. of Cider Vinegar

Directions:

- Remove the seeds and the cores from your peppers.

- Prepare the sauce by blending all of the ingredients together in a blender.

- Simmer it on low heist for 15 minutes. Stir in the vinegar.

- Heat 1 inch of the coconut oil in a heavy pan to 365°F/185°C.

- Using a whisk, stir the flour, baking powder, salt, and paprika in a bowl.

- Add in the water and whisk it until the batter is very smooth. Put it aside.

- In a different bowl, mix the breadcrumbs and the coconut to make a coating for the shrimp.

- One by one, add the shrimp to the batter and then roll it in the coconut mix.

- When the oil is hot, fry the shrimp in batches until they are golden brown. Turn the shrimp once.

- Remove it from the oil with a slotted spoon. Allow them to drain on paper towels.

Nutritional Information:

Calories: 74

Total Fat: 2g

Saturated Fat: 1g

Carbohydrates: 5g

Protein: 3g

Catfish Soup

Ingredients:

- 250g of Catfish – 1 inch/"cm Chunks, Deboned
- 500ml of Fish Stock
- 250ml of Coconut Milk
- 1 Tbsp. of Lemon Grass – Sliced Thin
- 1 Tbsp. of Cilantro Leaves
- 1 Tbsp. of Thai Chile Peppers – Sliced Thin
- 1 Tbsp. of Galangal – Sliced Thin
- 1 Clove of Garlic – Minced
- 4 Tbsp. of Fish Sauce
- 4 Tbsp. of Lime Juice

Directions:

- Combine all of the ingredients except for the fish and the coconut milk into a stockpot.

- Bring it to a boil for at least 1 minute.

- Reduce the heat and simmer it on low for 5 minutes.

- Add in the coconut milk and the fish.

- Simmer it for 10 minutes.

Nutritional Information:

Calories: 201

Total Fat: 12g

Saturated Fat: 3g

Carbohydrates: 7g

Protein: 16g

Breaded Coconut Fish

Ingredients:

- 500g of Fish – Tilapia, River Fish, Etc.
- 250g of Shredded Coconut
- 120ml of Coconut Oil
- 1 Box of Crackers
- 1 tsp. of Salt
- 1 tsp. of Pepper

Directions:

- Preheat your oven to 400°F/200°C.
- In a zip lock bag, put the fish and oil in and allow it to sit while you grind the crackers to powder.
- Add in the coconut, pepper, and the salt.
- Add the dry mix to the bag and shake it.
- In a baking dish, use the rest of the oil and scoop out enough of the extra mix to put on the bottom of the dish.
- Layer your fish and cover it with the rest of the dry mix.
- Put dish in the oven for 20-30 minutes and cook it on each side until it is brown.

Nutritional Information:

Calories: 47

Total Fat: 2g

Saturated Fat: 0g

Carbohydrates: 1g

Protein: 7g

Shrimp and Carrot Quinoa

Ingredients:

- Olive Oil
- 170g of Quinoa
- 500ml of Chicken Stock
- 3 Tbsp. of Coconut Flakes
- 25g of Grated Carrots
- 40g of Diced Onion
- 1 tsp. of Ginger – Grated
- ½ tsp. of Minced Garlic
- 10 Deveined Shrimp
- Lime Juice
- Cilantro – Garnish

Directions:

- Cook the stock and the quinoa using the directions on the package.

- Toast the coconut flakes in a medium sized pan and set it aside.

- Coat a large pan with olive oil and sauté the carrots and onions until they are tender.

- Add the ginger and the garlic and cook for another minute. Set it aside.

- In the same pan, sauté the shrimp until it is brown.

- When the quinoa is cooked, toss the coconut flakes, onions, carrots, ginger, and garlic into it.

- Add in the minced cilantro and the lime juice.

- Top it with the shrimp.

Nutritional Information:

- Calories: 210

- Total Fat: 23g

- Saturated Fat: 7g

- Carbohydrates: 76g

- Protein: 20g

Coconut Shrimp Curry

Ingredients:

- 2 Tbsp. of Butter

- 750g of Shrimp

- 1 Medium Onion – Finely Diced

- 4 Minced Cloves of Garlic

- 1 Tbsp. of Powdered Curry

- 250ml of Coconut Milk

- 2 Tbsp. of Honey

- ¼ tsp. of Salt

- Lime Juice

- Hot Sauce

- 12 Basil Leaves

- 450g of Basmati Rice – Cooked

Directions:

- In a large pan over medium heat, add the butter.

- Cook the shrimp on each side for 3 minutes. (Cook until they are opaque.) Set them aside.

- Add in the onion, garlic, and ginger into the pan.

- Sprinkle the curry on the top.

- Add in the coconut milk and stir the mixture.

- Add the lime juice, hot sauce, and honey.

- Cook it on medium heat until it bubbles.

- Add the shrimp and the basil. Allow it to cook for another minute.

- Put a spoonful of shrimp mixture over the rice.

Nutritional Information:

Calories: 210

Total Fat: 23g

Saturated Fat: 16g

Carbohydrates: 63g

Protein: 29g

Spicy Garlic Shrimp

Ingredients:

- 320g of Long Grain Rice
- 500g of Jumbo Shrimp – Peeled, Deveined
- 6 Large Minced Garlic Cloves
- 330ml of Water
- Dash of Salt
- 1 Jalapeno – De-Ribbed, De-Seeded
- 1 Lime
- 1 Tbsp. of Olive Oil
- 160ml of Coconut Milk
- 1 Tsp. of Red Chili Powder
- Cilantro

Directions:

- Cook the rice according to the package directions.

- In a blender, chop the garlic with water and ½ teaspoon of salt. Make sure there are still bits of garlic; a few pulses should do.

- Pour the mixture over the shrimp and let it sit for 10 minutes.

- Strain the water away from the shrimp and the garlic.

- Add in the lime juice, ½ teaspoon of salt, and jalapeno.

- Heat one tablespoon of olive oil over high heat in a large pan.

- Add in the shrimp and cook it for one minute.

- Add one small can of coconut milk and cook it for another 30 seconds.

- Mix the chili powder into the mixture.

- Put the rice in a large bowl.

- Mix in the the coconut milk into the rice.

- Serve the shrimp over the rice and garnish it with cilantro.

Nutritional Information:

Calories: 610

Total Fat: 18g

Saturated Fat: 10g

Carbohydrates: 77g

Protein: 34g

Sweet Chili Coconut Shrimp

Ingredients:

- 230g of Mayonnaise

- 2 Tbsp. of Sweet Chili Sauce

- 1 tsp. of Hot Sauce

- 500g of Shrimp – Shelled, keep tail

- 55g of Flour

- 1 Egg

- 2 Tbsp. of Coconut Milk

- Dash of Salt

- Dash of Pepper

- 45g of Panko Breadcrumbs

- 30g of Sweetened Coconut Flakes

- Frying Oil

Directions:

- In a small mixing bowl, add the sweet chili sauce, mayonnaise, and hot sauce.

- Using a paring knife, cut down the deep of the middle part of the back of the shrimp; discard the black vein.

- In three shallow bowls, put flour in one, whisk the egg in another, and put the coconut in the last one.

- Combine the panko to the coconut flakes.

- In a large frying pan, add in 2 inches/5cm of oil and heat it over medium heat until it is 350°F/180°C.

- While the oil heats, dip the shrimp in the flour and shake off the excess.

- Dip the shrimp into the egg, then the coconut flakes.

- Fry the shrimp in smaller batches for 3 minutes until it is golden brown on both sides.

- Serve the shrimp with sweet chili mayo for shrimp dipping.

Nutritional Information:

- Calories: 410

- Total Fat: 22g

- Saturated Fat: 9g

- Carbohydrates: 26g

- Protein: 28g

Thai Shrimp

Ingredients:

- 750g of Unpeeled Raw Shrimp – Large

Coconut Lime Rice

- 3 Tbsp. of Lime Juice

- 2 Tbsp. of Dry Roasted Peanuts – Unsalted

- 2 Tbsp. of Ginger

- 2 Minced Cloves of Garlic

- 1 tsp. of Salt

- 2 tsp. of Honey

- ½ tsp. of Red Pepper – Crushed

- 60ml of Olive Oil

- 90g of Coconut

Directions:

- Peel and devein the shrimp.

- Put the oil, lime juice, peanuts, ginger, coconut, garlic, salt, and honey into a food processor. (For 20 seconds.)

- Sauté the shrimp with 1 Tbsp. of oil in a large frying pan. It will take 3-5 minutes.

- Stir the cilantro mixture into the shrimp and serve over the rice.

Nutritional Information:

Calories: 300

Total Fat: 13.9g

Saturated Fat: 3.7g

Carbohydrates: 23.9g

Protein: 21g

Thai Halibut

Ingredients:

- 2 tsp. of Vegetable Oil

- 4 Shallots – Finely Chopped

- 2 ½ tsp. of Red Curry Paste

- 500ml of Low Sodium Chicken Broth

- 130ml of Light Coconut Milk

- ½ tsp. of Salt

- Dash of Salt

- 150g Halibut Fillets – Remove Skin

- A few Spinach Leaves – Steamed

- 25g of Chopped Cilantro

- 2 Scallions – Green Only – Sliced Thin

- 2 Tbsp. of Lime Juice

- Dash of Black Pepper

- 450g of Brown Rice – Cooked

Directions:

- Cook the rice per package instructions.

- Steam fresh spinach leaves in the microwave for 2 minutes.

- Using a large sauté pan, heat the olive oil on medium heat.

- Add shallots and cook them until they are brown. Stir them occasionally.

- Add the curry paste and continue cooking them until it is fragrant; 30 seconds.

- Add in the chicken broth, ½ tsp. of slat, and coconut milk. Simmer it. This will take 5 minutes.

- Season the halibut with a dash of salt.

- Arrange the fish inside the pan.

- Gently shake the sauté pan in order to coat the fish with the sauce.

- Cover the halibut and cook it until the fish flakes easily using a fork. This will take 7 minutes.

- Arrange a pile of spinach in the bottom of a soup plate.

- Top the spinach with fish fillets.

- Stir the scallions' cilantro, and lime juice into the sauce.

- Ladle the sauce on top of the fish and serve it with rice.

Nutritional Information:

Calories: 634

Total Fat: 9g

Saturated Fat: 8g

Carbohydrates: 10g

Protein: 21g

Thai-Mex-Coconut Snapper

Ingredients:

- 750g of Boneless Red Snapper Fillets
- 2 Tbsp. of Vegetable Oil –Divided
- 1 Pasilla Chili Pepper – Dried
- 1 Onion – Medium, Chopped
- 1 Red Bell Pepper – Chopped
- 90g of Chiitake Mushrooms – Sliced
- 1 ½ tsp. of Grated Ginger
- 2 tsp. of Garlic – Chopped
- 1 Chili De Arbol – Chopped
- 120ml of Coconut Milk
- 60g of Mayonnaise
- 2 tsp. of Chicken Bouillon
- 120ml of Water

Directions:

- Remove the stem and the seeds from the chile. Toast it in a dry skillet on medium heat. (Press it down with a spatula.)

- Pour boiling water on the chili. Cover it and allow it to soak 10 minutes.

- Process the pasilla chile with the soaking liquid in a small food processor and set it aside.

- Sprinkle the snapper with the bouillon. Heat 1 Tbsp. of oil in a 12 inch/30cm deep skillet on medium-high heat.

- Cook the snapper with the flesh side down until it is golden. This will take 3 minutes.

- Heat the remaining 1 Tbsp. of oil in the same skillet and cook the red pepper, onion, and mushrooms; stir it frequently.

- Stir in the ginger, chile, and garlic; cook it for 30 seconds.

- Stir in the pasilla chili puree and cook it; stir it occasionally, until it is thick. (2 Minutes)

- Stir in the coconut milk and water. Bring it to a boil on high heat.

- Reduce the heat to low and add in the snapper.

- Simmer the snapper until it flakes; 5 minutes.

- Gently whisk in the mayonnaise.

Nutritional Information:

Calories: 270

Total Fat: 17g

Saturated Fat: 5g

Carbohydrates: 5g

Protein: 25g

Coconut Shrimp

Ingredients:

- 1x – 360g Package of Coconut Shrimp

- 70g of Mayonnaise

- 5 Slices of Muenster Cheese – Cut in half and then fold it over

- Green Leaf Lettuce – Tear into 10 pieces.

- 10 Party Sized Potato Rolls – Split

Directions:

- Cook the coconut shrimp using the package directions. Remove the tails.

- Combine 2 Tbsp. of mayonnaise with the dipping sauce included in the coconut shrimp package.

- Evenly spread the rolls with the mixture.

- Add a piece of lettuce to the rolls, then the shrimp and cheese.

- Push a toothpick through the top and garnish with a cube of mango, pineapple, or papaya.

Nutritional Information:

Calories: 200

Total Fat: 10g

Saturated Fat: 1g

Carbohydrates: 35g

Protein: 4g

Honey Coconut Salmon

Ingredients:

- 320g of Butter

- 270g of Honey

- 70g of Brown Sugar

- 45g of Flake Coconut

- 4x – 120g Salmon Fillets

Directions:

- Melt the butter in a medium saucepan on medium heat.

- Mix in the brown sugar, honey, and coconut.

- Bring the mixture to a boil and then remove it from the heat. Allow it to cool slightly.

- Put the mixture in a large mixing bowl.

- Put the salmon in the bowl and turn it to thoroughly goat the salmon.

- Cover the bowl and allow it to sit in the refrigerator for 30 minutes.

- Preheat your oven to 375°F/190°C.

- Spread the marinade mix in a baking dish in order to coat the bottom.

- Arrange the salmon onto the dish and pour some of the marinade on top.

- Bake the fish for 25 minutes. Bat it occasionally.

Nutritional Information:

Calories: 1040

Total Fat: 77g

Saturated Fat: 49g

Carbohydrates: 69g

Protein: 24g

Grilled Shrimp

Ingredients:

- 3 Cloves of Garlic – Mined
- 80ml of Coconut Oil
- 55g of Tomato Sauce
- 2 Tbsp. of Red Wine Vinegar
- 2 Tbsp. of Basil
- ½ tsp. of Salt
- ¼ tsp. of Cayenne Pepper
- 1kg of Shrimp – Peeled, De-Veined
- Skewers

Directions:

- In a large mixing bowl, stir together coconut oil, garlic, tomato sauce, and vinegar.

- Season with salt, basil, and pepper.

- Add the shrimp to the bowl, and stir it until all the shrimp was covered.

- Cover the shrimp and refrigerate it for 30 minute to 1 hour.

- Preheat the grill over medium heat.

- Thread the shrimp onto the skewers, piercing once near the head, and then through the tail.

- Lightly oil the grill grate.

- Cook the shrimp on the grill for 2-3 minutes on each side.

Nutritional Information:

Calories: 416

Total Fat: 22g

Saturated Fat: 12g

Carbohydrates: 41g

Protein: 15g

Grilled Alaska Salmon

Ingredients:

- 8x – 120g Salmon – Fillet
- 120ml of Coconut Oil
- 4 Tbsp. of Soy Sauce
- 4 Tbsp. Of Balsamic Vinegar
- 4 Tbsp. of Green Onions – Chopped
- 3 tsp. of Brown Sugar
- 2 Cloves of Garlic – Minced
- 1 ½ tsp. of Ground Ginger
- 2 tsp. of Red Pepper Flakes
- 1 tsp. of Sesame Oil
- ½ tsp. of Salt

Directions:

- Place the filets in a medium glass dish.

- In a medium-mixing bowl, combine the oil, soy sauce, green onions, vinegar, brown sugar, ginger, garlic, pepper, salt, and sesame oil. Whisk it together thoroughly.

- Pour it over the fish and cover it. Allow it to sit in the refrigerator for 4-6 hours.

- Prepare the grill with coals 5 inches/13cm away from the grate.

- Grill the fish for 5 inches/13cm from the coals for 10 minutes for each inch of thickness.

Nutritional Information:

Calories: 280

Total Fat: 13g

Saturated Fat: 3g

Carbohydrates: 0g

Protein: 39g

Seared Salmon and Braised Broccoli

Ingredients:

- 600g of Alaskan Salmon Fillet – Skinned, Cut to 4 Portions

- 1 Tbsp. of Rosemary

- 1 tsp. of Salt

- 2 Heads of Broccoli

- 1 ½ Tbsp. of Olive Oil – Divided

- 1 Small Onion – Diced

- 3 Tbsp. of Raisins

- 2 Tbsp. of Pine Nuts

- 120ml of Water

Directions:

- Season the salmon with half of the rosemary and ½ tsp. of salt 20 minutes before you cook it.

- Cut the broccoli into florets with 2 inch/4cm stalks.

- Remove the outer layer of the stalk with a peeler. Cut your florets in half (lengthwise).

- Heat one tablespoon of oil in a large pan on medium heat.

- Add the onion and cook it 3-4 minutes.

- Add in the raisins, rosemary, and pine nuts. Toss it to coat it very well.

- Cook it for 3-5 minutes.

- Add in the broccoli, salt, and then toss it.

- Add in the water and bring it to boil.

- Reduce the heat to a simmer and then cook it for 8-10 minutes.

- Heat the rest of the oil in a pan on medium high heat.

- Add the salmon with the skin side up and then cook it for 3-5 minutes.

- Turn the salmon over and then remove it from the pan. Allow it to stand for 3-5 minutes.

- Divide the broccoli for every piece of salmon.

Nutritional Information:

Calories: 311

Total Fat: 14g

Saturated Fat: 2g

Carbohydrates: 16g

Protein: 32g

Orange Sesame Shrimp

Ingredients:

- 3 Tbsp. of Sesame Seeds

- 2 Large Egg Whites

- 30g of Cornstarch

- ¼ tsp. of Salt

- ¼ tsp. of Pepper

- 500g of Shrimp – Peeled, Deveined

- 2 Tbsp. of Canola Oil – Divided

- 200ml of Orange Juice

- 60ml of Dry Sherry

- 2 Tbsp. of Soy Sauce – Reduced Sodium

- 1 tsp. of Sweetener

- 1 Scallion – Sliced Thin

Directions:

- Whisk the sesame seeds, cornstarch, egg white, pepper, and salt in a large mixing bowl.

- Add in the shrimp and then toss it to coat it well.

- Heat one tablespoon of the oil in a large pan on medium heat.

- Add in half of the shrimp and cook it for 1-2 minutes on both sides.

- Transfer it to a plate that is lined with paper towels.

- Repeat it with the rest of the oil and the shrimp.

- Ad din the orange juice, soy sauce, sherry, and sweetener to the pan.

- Boil it and cook for 4-6 minutes.

- Return the shrimp to the same pan and stir it to coat it with the sauce.

- Serve it immediately with the scallions sprinkled on top.

Nutritional Information:

Calories: 249

Total Fat: 10g

Saturated Fat: 1g

Carbohydrates: 13g

Protein: 22g

Halibut Mushrooms and Polenta

Ingredients:

- 1 Tbsp. of Virgin Olive Oil

- 4 Slices of Bacon – Cooked, Chopped

- 150g of Red Onion – Sliced

- 240g of Mushrooms – Sliced

- 60ml of White Wine

- 1x – 500g of Polenta – Tube, Sliced into 8 Rounds

- 150g Halibut – Skinned

- ¼ tsp. of Salt

- ¼ tsp. of Pepper

- 2 tbsp. of Basil

Directions:

- Preheat the oven to 450°F/230°C.

- Tear off four sheets of some parchment paper or foil. Spray it if you're using foil.

- Heat the oil in a large pan on medium high heat.

- Add in the bacon and cook it until its soft, 2-3 minutes.

- Add in the onion and garlic.

- Cook it for 2 minutes.

- Stir in the mushrooms and cook it for 4-7 minutes.

- Add in the wine and scrape up the browned bits. Remove it from the heat.

- In order to make a packet, set one of the sheets of the parchment long side closest to you. Fold it in half from the short end, and then open it like a book.

- Place 2 slices of the polenta on one side. Set the fillet on the polentas and sprinkle it with salt and pepper.

- Divide the mushroom mix among the packets. Spoon it over your fish. Close the packets and seal the edges with the small and tight folds.

- Place the packets on your large baking sheet. Bake the packets until your fish is cooked. This will take about 14 minutes.

- Set the packets on the plates. Cut an X in the top of the packets with some scissors. Carefully fold it open. Serve it with the basil on top.

Nutritional Information:

Calories: 298

Total Fat: 15g

Saturated Fat: 2g

Carbohydrates: 9g

Protein: 32g

Fish Fillets and Pineapple Jalapeno Salsa

Ingredients:
Salsa

- 1 Small Pineapple

- 25g of Scallions – Minced

- 3 Tbsp. of Cilantro – Chopped

- 3 Tbsp. of Lime Juice

- 2 Tbsp. of Jalapeno – Minced

- ¼ tsp. of Salt

- Dash of Pepper

Fish

- 40g of Flour

- ½ tsp. of Salt

- ¼ tsp. of Pepper

- 500g of Catfish – Cut into 4 Portions

- 1 Tbsp. of Virgin Olive Oil

Directions:

- Salsa: Cut the top off of the pineapple and skin it. Remove the eyes and the core. Dice it finely and put it in a medium mixing bowl. Add in the scallions, lime juice, cilantro, jalapeno, and the oil. Toss it to mix it. Season it with ¼ tsp. of salt and pepper.

- Fish: Combine the flour, ½ tsp. of salt, and ¼ tsp. of pepper in a shallow dish or plate. Dredge the fillets through it.

- Heat he oil in a large pan on medium high heat.

- Add in the fish and cook it until it is browned. This will take about 3-4 minutes on each side. Serve it with the salsa.

Nutritional Information:

Calories: 192

Total Fat: 9g

Saturated Fat: 2g

Carbohydrates: 14g

Protein: 13g

Baked Cod and Chorizo with White Beans

Ingredients:

- 1 tsp. of Virgin Olive Oil

- 1 Shallot – Chopped Fine

- 60g of Spanish Chorizo

- 1 tsp. of Thyme

- 500g of Grape Tomatoes – Halved

- 120ml of Dry White Wine – Divided

- 1x – 450g Can of Northern Beans – Rinsed

- ½ tsp. of Salt – Divided

- 600g of Cod – Cut to 4 pieces

- Dash of Pepper

Directions:

- Preheat your oven to 425°F/220°C.

- Coat a 9x13inch/23x33cm-baking dish with cooking oil.

- Heat the oil in a medium pan on medium high heat.

- Add in the shallot, thyme, and chorizo. Cook it for 1 minute.

- Add in the tomatoes and wine. Cook it for 2-4 minutes.

- Stir in the beans and ¼ tsp. of salt and then remove it from the heat.

- Sprinkle the fish with the rest of the salt and pepper. Put it in the baking dish.

- Top the fish with the tomato mix.

- Pour in the rest of the wine in a pan and cover it with foil.

- Bake it for 15-20 minutes.

- Serve the fish and the sauce on top.

Nutritional Information:

Calories: 293

Total Fat: 8g

Saturated Fat: 2g

Carbohydrates: 18g

Protein: 30g

Grilled Salmon with Herbs

Ingredients:

- 2 Lemons – Sliced Thinly
- 1 Lemon – Cut to Edges for Garnish
- 20-30 Sprigs of Fresh Herbs
- 2 Tbsp. of Chopped Herb – Divided
- 1 Clove of Garlic - Mashed
- ¼ tsp. of Salt
- 1 Tbsp. of Dijon Mustard
- 500g of Salmon – Skinned

Directions:

- Preheat your grill on medium high heat.

- Lay two pieces of foil on the top of a baking sheet.

- Arrange the lemon slices in two layers in the middle of the foil.

- Spread the herb sprigs on the lemons.

- Mash the garlic with the salt in order to create a paste.

- Transfer it to a small bowl and stir in the mustard and the rest of the chopped herbs.

- Spread the mix on both sides of your salmon.

- Place the salmon on top of the sprigs.

- Slide the foil off of the baking sheet onto the grill with the foil.

- Cover the grill and allow it to cook for 18-24 minutes.

- Wearing your oven mitts, transfer the foil and the salmon back on the baking sheet.

- Cut the salmon into portions and then serve it with the lemon wedges.

Nutritional Information:

Calories: 212

Total Fat: 12g

Saturated Fat: 2g

Carbohydrates: 1g

Protein: 23g

Grilled Lime and Honey Salmon

Ingredients:

- 500g of Salmon – Boneless, Skinless
- 1 Tbsp. of Soy Sauce
- 2 Tbsp. of Lime Juice
- 1 Tbsp. of Honey
- ½ tsp. of Lime Zest

Directions:

- Preheat your grill.
- Whisk the soy sauce, honey, lime juice, and the lime zest in a small mixing bowl.
- Put the salmon on a covered baking dish (cover it with aluminum foil).
- Brush your salmon with the honey lime sauce and allow it to sit for 15 minutes.
- Cook if for 3-4 minutes on each side.

Nutritional Information:

Calories: 216

Total Fat: 8g

Saturated Fat: 2g

Carbohydrates: 5g

Protein: 30g

Jalapeno Salmon

Ingredients:

- 500g of Salmon – Boneless, Skinless
- 1 Jalapeno
- 2 Tbsp. of Cilantro
- 70g of Hard Cheese – Reduced Fat
- Juice from 1 Lime
- ½ tsp. of Cumin
- ½ tsp. of Garlic Powder
- ½ tsp. of Onion Powder
- Salt
- Pepper

Directions:

- Chop up 2/3 the salmon and add it to the food processor.

- Chop the rest of the salmon into 1/3 chunk.

- Add in the jalapeno and the cilantro to the processor and then pulse a few times. It should be thick.

- Combine the salmon with the cheese, cumin, lime juice, garlic powder, and the onion powder.

- Form the mix into patties and then put it in the freezer for at least 15 minutes.

- Heat a pan on medium high heat.

- Spray the pan and then add in the patties. Cook them for 4-5 minutes on both sides.

Nutritional Information:

Calories: 246

Total Fat: 12g

Saturated Fat: 3g

Carbohydrates: 8g

Protein: 8g

Spicy Seared Shrimp

Ingredients:

- 240g of Cellophane Noodles
- 120ml of Chicken Broth- Reduced Sodium
- 2 Tbsp. of Soy Sauce – Reduced Sodium
- 2 tsp. of Cornstarch
- 1 tsp. of Red Pepper Flakes
- 1 Tbsp. of Peanut Oil
- 1 Tbsp. of Ginger – Minced
- 4 Cloves of Garlic – Mined
- 1.5kg of Shrimp – Peeled, Deveined
- 25g of Scallions – Chopped

Directions:

- Soak the cellophane noodles in hot water for about 10 minutes until they are soft.

- Drain the noodles and set them aside.

- In a small mixing bowl, whisk the broth, soy sauce, red pepper flakes, and cornstarch together and set them aside.

- Heat the oil in your wok on medium high heat.

- Add in the ginger and the garlic and cook it for 1 minute.

- Add in the shrimp and cook it for 2-3 minutes until they are pink.

- Add in the broth mix and cook it for 1 minute until the shrimp is cooked through and the sauce thickens.

- Remove it from the heat and stir in the scallions.

- Serve half of the shrimp on the noodles with the sauce.

Nutritional Information:

Calories: 121

Total Fat: 7g

Saturated Fat: 1g

Carbohydrates: 6g

Protein: 9g

Sherry Shrimp Stir Fry

Ingredients:

- 500g of Shrimp – Deveined
- 500g of Broccoli - Chopped
- 250g of Carrots – Sliced
- 4 Green Onions – Chopped
- 1 tsp. of Ginger – Minced
- 1 tsp. of Garlic – Minced
- 10 Tbsp. of Soy Sauce
- 2 Tbsp. of Cooking Sherry
- 2 Tbsp. of Sugar
- 2 Tbsp. of Cornstarch

Directions:

- Soak your shrimp in salt water until they are defrosted.
- Devein and marinate them with garlic, sesame oil, and ginger.
- Mix the soy sauce, sugar, sherry, and cornstarch. Set it aside.
- Stir fry the vegetables and then add in the shrimp until they are pink.
- Add the sauce and they let stand for 2-5 minutes.

Nutritional Information:

- Calories: 248
- Total Fat: 2g
- Saturated Fat: 0g
- Carbohydrates: 28g
- Protein: 29g

Shrimp, Broccoli, Sprout Stir Fry

Ingredients:

- 10 Large Sized Shrimp

- 150g of Onions – Chopped

- 175 of Broccoli – Chopped

- 110g of Bok Choy – Chopped

- 200g of Bean Sprouts

- 25g of Carrots – Sliced

- 1 Tbsp. of Olive Oil

- 130g of Rice

- 330ml of Chicken Broth

Directions:

- Sauté the onions, carrots, and the broccoli in half of the olive oil.

- Cook it until it is done. Then put aside.

- Add in the rest of the oil in the pan, stir in the rice on low heat.

- Add in the chicken broth and stir it regularly.

- Add in the rest of the liquid ingredients and then cover the rice and allow it to finish cooking.

- Add in the shrimp and the vegetables that were cooked.

- Stir it well on low heat.

- Add in a small amount of water to ensure it does not burn. Cover it until the shrimp are pink.

- Add the bok choy and the bean sprouts. Mix it well.

Nutritional Information:

Calories: 393

Total Fat: 9g

Saturated Fat: 2g

Carbohydrates: 57g

Protein: 22g

Salmon Stir Fry

Ingredients:

- 90g of Salmon

- 90g of Broccoli – Chopped

- 15g of Carrots – Sliced

- ½ tsp. of Ginger – Minced

- ½ tsp. of Garlic – minced

- 3 Tbsp. of Soy Sauce

- 1 Tbsp. of Olive Oil

- 2 tsp. of Sugar

- 130g of White Rice

Directions:

- Defrost the salmon fillets and marinate it with the garlic, ½ Tbsp. of olive oil, and the ginger.

- Mix the soy sauce and the sugar in a bowl and put it aside.

- Prepare the rice like it says on the package.

- Stir-fry the vegetables and the salmon in the rest of the olive oil.

- Pour the stir-fry on the rice and allow it to stand for 2-4 minutes.

Nutritional Information:

Calories: 362

Total Fat: 13g

Saturated Fat: 2g

Carbohydrates: 46g

Protein: 15g

Shrimp and Chinese Noodle Stir Fry

Ingredients:

- 500g of Shrimp
- 240g of Chinese Noodles
- 75g of Onion – Chopped
- 50g of Celery – Sliced
- 1 tsp. of Salt
- 240g of Snow Peas
- 6 Tbsp. of Sesame Oil
- 4 Tbsp. of Soy Sauce
- 2 tsp. of Cooking Wine
- ½ tsp. of Sugar
- 2 tsp. of Cornstarch

Directions:

- Cook the noodles by boiling in water until they are soft.

- Drain the water and add in 3 Tbsp. of sesame oil. Put them aside.

- Peel the shrimp and coat them with cornstarch.

- Add in 3 Tbsp. of sesame oil in the wok and fry the noodles until they are the texture of your choosing.

- Add in the snow peas, celery, onion, shrimp, and the sauce.

- Add in the 4 Tbsp. of soy sauce, 2 tsp. of cooking wine, 1 tsp. of salt, and ½ tsp. of sugar.

Nutritional Information:

Calories: 641

Total Fat: 40g

Saturated Fat: 6g

Carbohydrates: 41g

Protein: 31g

Seafood Stir Fry

Ingredients:

- 120ml of Vegetable Broth
- 240g of Shrimp – Peeled, Deveined
- 240g of Sea Scallops
- 3 Carrots – Julienned
- 4 Celery Stalks – Sliced
- 2 Red Bell Peppers – Seeded, Julienned
- 2 Yellow Bell Peppers – Seeded, Julienned
- 2 Green Bell Peppers – Seeded, Julienned
- 200g of Bean Sprouts
- 12 Mushrooms – Sliced
- 3 tsp. of Garlic – Minced
- 50g of Cilantro – Chopped
- 8 Scallions – Cut to 1 inch/2cm Pieces
- 2 Fruit Limes – Juiced
- 1 tsp. of Red Pepper Flakes
- 60ml of Balsamic Vinegar

Directions:

- In your wok, heat up the oil until it starts to smoke.

- Add the scallops and the shrimp. Sauté them for about 3 minutes.

- Add in the celery, carrots, bell peppers, garlic, and mushrooms.

- Sauté them for 3 minutes.

- Add in the lime juice, the pepper flakes, and the sherry.

- Mix in the ingredients and cook them for 1 minute.

- Add in the soy sauce and mix it all together.

Nutritional Information:

Calories: 252

Total Fat: 3g

Saturated Fat: 0g

Carbohydrates: 30g

Protein: 30g

Seafood Stir Fry

Ingredients:

- 250g of Shrimp – Peeled, Deveined
- 250g of Scallops
- 2 Medium Sized Carrots – Cut to Matchsticks
- 330g of Bok Choy – Chopped
- 1 Bunch of Green Onions – Chopped
- 1 Onion – Chopped
- 175g of Broccoli – Chopped
- 1 Can (about 200g) of Whole Water Chestnuts
- Soy Sauce
- 240g of Clam Juice
- 1 Can (about 200ml) of De-Fatted Chicken Broth
- 2 Cloves of Garlic – Minced
- 3 Tbsp. of Cornstarch
- 75g of Mushrooms – Sliced
- 3-4 Tbsp. of Olive Oil
- 100g of Bean Sprouts
- 150g of Snow Peas

Directions:

- Sauté all ingredients in your wok for 2-3 minutes.

- Make sure all of the shrimp that are in the wok are pink.

Nutritional Information:

Calories: 248

Total Fat: 2g

Saturated Fat: 0g

Carbohydrates: 21g

Protein: 13g

Garlic Shrimp with Noodle Stir Fry

Ingredients:

- 180g of Brown Rice Noodles
- 2 Tbsp. of Rice Vinegar
- 1 ½ Tbsp. of Soy Sauce – low Sodium
- 1 Tbsp. of Honey
- 1 tsp. of Fish Sauce
- ½ tsp. of Cornstarch
- 650g of Shrimp
- 1 ½ tsp. of Canola Oil
- 50g of Cashews – Unsalted
- 3 Cloves of Garlic – Crushed
- ½ Jalapeno – Sliced
- 1 Tbsp. of Canola Oil
- 25g of Carrots – Julienned
- 150g of Green Onions – Chopped
- 180g of Baby Spinach

Directions:

- Boil the noodles until they are done. Drain and rinse them with cold water.

- Combine the vinegar, honey, soy sauce, fish sauce, and the cornstarch.

- Add in the shrimp.

- Heat it with 1 ½ tsp. of canola oil in a large wok on high heat.

- Add the cashews, garlic, and the jalapeno peppers. Stir-fry it for 30 seconds.

- Remove the mix from the wok.

- Add 1 Tbsp. of canola oil into the wok.

- Add in the green onions, carrots, and the bell peppers. Stir-fry it for 3 minutes.

- Add the noodles, cashew mix, shrimp mix, and the spinach. Cook it for 1-½ minutes.

Nutritional Information:

Calories: 424

Total Fat: 14g

Saturated Fat: 2g

Carbohydrates: 57g

Protein: 19g

Thai Shrimp with Eggplant Stir Fry

Ingredients:

- 2 Tbsp. of Lime Juice
- 1 ½ Tbsp. of Asian Fish Sauce
- 1 ½ tsp. of Sugar
- 1 Tbsp. of Peanut Oil
- 5 tsp. of Peanut Oil
- 500g of Large Shrimp – Peeled, Deveined
- 3 Slender Japanese Eggplants – Halved, Then Cut in Half
- 5 Cloves of Garlic – Sliced Thin
- 2 Fresno Chilies – Seeded, Slivered
- 1 Scallion – Sliced Thin
- A Handful of Torn Basil Leaves
- Lime Wedges
- Cooked Rice Noodles

Directions:

- In a small mixing bowl, whisk together the fish sauce, lime juice, sugar, and 2 Tbsp. of water.

- In a wok, heat 1 Tbsp. of oil on medium high heat until it is hot.

- Add in the shrimp and stir-fry it until they are pink, it will be 3 minutes.

- Transfer it to a bowl.

- Add in 2 tsp. of oil and half of the eggplant in the wok.

- Cook it for 2 minutes then stir-fry it for 30 seconds.

- Transfer it to a bowl with the shrimp.

- Add in another 2 tsp. of oil.

- Repeat it with the rest of the eggplant.

- Add in another 1 tsp. of oil, chilies, garlic, and the scallions. Stir-fry it until it is fragrant for 1 minute.

- Add in the shrimp, eggplant, and the sauce to the wok.

- Cook it for another 30 seconds.

- Stir in the basil. Serve it with the lime wedges and rice noodles.

Nutritional Information:

Calories: 209

Total Fat: 10g

Saturated Fat: 2g

Carbohydrates: 12g

Protein: 18g

Ginger Shrimp Stir Fry

Ingredients:

- 500g of Medium Sized Shrimp – Peeled, Deveined
- 1 tsp. of Ginger – Peeled, Minced
- ½ tsp. of Salt
- Dash of White Pepper
- 120ml of Water
- 1 Tbsp. of Mirin
- 2 tsp. of Soy Sauce – Low Sodium
- 1 ½ tsp. of Cornstarch
- 1 tsp. of Sugar
- 1 tsp. of Dark Sesame Oil
- ½ tsp. of Chile Paste with Garlic
- 1 Tbsp. of Canola Oil – Divided
- 150g of Onion – Sliced Thin
- 4 Cloves of Garlic – Minced
- 100g of Celery – Sliced

Directions:

- Put the shrimp in a medium sized bowl.

- Sprinkle it with ginger, pepper, and salt.

- Toss it and let it stand for 5 minutes.

- Combine water and the next 6 ingredients in a small bowl. Stir it with a whisk.

- Heat 1 tsp. of canola oil in a large wok on medium high heat.

- Add the shrimp mix to a wok, stir-fry it for 2 minutes.

- Remove the shrimp mix from the wok and set it aside.

- Wipe a pan dry with a paper towel.

- Heat the 2 tsp. of canola oil in a wok on medium high heat.

- Add the onion and the garlic and stir-fry it for 1 minute.

- Add the celery; stir-fry it for 1 minute.

- Return the shrimp mix to the wok and stir-fry it for 1 minute.

Nutritional Information:

Calories: 192

Total Fat: 7g

Saturated Fat: 1g

Carbohydrates: 7g

Protein: 23g

Scallop and Sugar Snap Pea Stir Fry

Ingredients:

- 360g of Sugar Snap Peas – Trimmed, Blanched

- 360g of Sea Scallops – Rinsed, Patted Dry

- 120ml of Chicken Broth – Fat Skimmed

- 2 Tbsp. of Mirin

- 1 Tbsp. of Cornstarch

- 2 Tbsp. of Vegetable Oil

- 2 Tbsp. of Green Onions – Sliced Thin

- 1 Tbsp. of Garlic – Minced

- ¼ tsp. of Hot Chile Flakes

- A Handful of Basil Leaves – Slivered

Directions:

- Cut the sugar snap peas in diagonal directions.

- Cut the scallops in half.

- In a small mixing bowl and whisk the broth, cornstarch, and mirin.

- Pour the oil in a wok and put it on high heat.

- Stir in the green onions, Chile flakes, and garlic. Stir it until it is fragrant.

- Add in the scallops and cook it for 2 minutes.

- Stir in the sugar snap peas and pour the broth mix. Cook it for 2-3 minutes.

- Stir in the basil. Pour it into a serving bowl.

Nutritional Information:

Calories: 210

Total Fat: 8g

Saturated Fat: 1g

Carbohydrates: 14g

Protein: 18g

Wok Seared Scallops

Ingredients:

- 175g of Butter

- Hot Pepper Sauce – Tabasco

- 24 Large Scallops

- Salt

- Pepper

- 500g of Sugar Snap Peas – Trimmed, Cleaned of Stems, Blanched

- 2 Red Bell Peppers – Diced

- Peanut Oil

- Teriyaki Sauce

Directions:

- Heat the wok on high heat.

- Working in batches, add in 2 tablespoons of butter and melt it.

- Add in a generous splash of Tabasco sauce.

- Add in four scallops to the butter mix and sear both sides of it until it is brown. About 1 minute per side.

- Season it with salt and pepper.

- Remove the scallops from the wok to a plate.

- Repeat it until it is all cooked.

- In the wok add the sugar peas and the bell peppers. Stir-fry it for 2-3 minutes until it is a bit soft.

- Dash it with teriyaki sauce. Give them a toss, and then serve it.

Nutritional Information:

Calories: 345

Total Fat: 9g

Saturated Fat: 2g

Carbohydrates: 24g

Protein: 14g

Seafood Wok and Rice

Ingredients:

- 30g of Snow Peas
- 15g of Chinese Potatoes
- 30g of Fresh Carrots
- 30g of Sliced Bamboo
- 30g of Celery
- 3 Scallops
- 3 Shrimp
- 90g of Fish – Cut to 1/3 inches/1cm
- 240g of Stock
- 2 Tbsp. of Peanut Oil
- Dash of Garlic
- Dash of Ginger
- 1 tsp. of Shoyu
- ¼ tsp. of sesame Oil
- 1 tsp. of Oyster Sauce
- ½ tsp. of Salt
- Dash of Ajinomoto
- ½ tsp. of Sugar
- 2 Crab Claws
- 60g of Saimin Noodles
- 150g of Rice Pilaf
- Parsley

Directions:

- Deep fry the noodles in a round basket and then put them on a platter.

- Heat your wok and add in the ginger, scallops, garlic, shrimp, and fish.

- Fry it until it is cooked.

- Add in the vegetables and stir-fry it for 3 minutes.

- Add the shoyu, oyster sauce, sesame oil, salt, sugar, and ajinomoto.

- Put the mix on the noodles.

- Add the crab claws on the mix.

Nutritional Information:

Calories: 435

Total Fat: 17g

Saturated Fat: 4g

Carbohydrates: 41g

Protein: 29g

Broccoli and Seafood Stir Fry

Ingredients:

- 15g of Ginger – Chopped
- 5 Cloves of Garlic – Minced
- 150g of Soy Sauce
- 120ml of Dry Sherry
- 1.5kg of Swordfish – Cut to Cubes
- 80ml of Peanut Oil
- 700g of Red Bell Pepper – Chopped
- 700g of Broccoli Flowerets – Blanched
- 300g of Snow Peas – Trimmed
- 200g of Scallions – Minced
- 500ml of Fish Stock
- 2 Tbsp. of Oyster Sauce
- 2 Tbsp. of Sesame Oil

Directions:

- Combine the first 4 ingredients with the swordfish. Marinate it for 20 minutes.

- Drain it and save the marinade.

- Heat oil in the wok until it begins to smoke.

- Add in the fish and cook it for 2 minutes.

- Remove the fish; wipe the wok clean.

- Add in the remaining oil and stir-fry the peppers and the broccoli for 2 minutes.

- Add the peas and the scallions and cook it for 1 minute.

- Add the fish marinade, oyster sauce, stock, and the sesame oil. Bring it to a boil.

- Optional: Serve it with rice.

Nutritional Information:

Calories: 410

Total Fat: 12g

Saturated Fat: 2g

Carbohydrates: 21g

Protein: 23g

Teriyaki Salmon Stir Fry

Ingredients:

- 60g of Teriyaki Sauce

- 2 tsp. of Sesame Oil

- 1 Tbsp. of Ginger – Finely Chopped

- 1 Clove of Garlic – Chipped Fine

- 500g of Salmon Filet – Skinned, Cut to Cubes

- 1 Tsp. of Vegetable Oil

- 300g of Mushrooms – Sliced

- 1 Head of Broccoli – Cut to Florets – Boiled for 2 Minutes and Cooled with Ice Water

- 1 Tbsp. of Sesame Seeds

Directions:

- In a baking dish, combine the teriyaki sauce, ginger, garlic, and sesame oil.

- Add the salmon and toss it to coat it. Allow it to sit for 10 minutes.

- Heat the oil in your wok until it begins to smoke.

- Stir in the mushrooms and toss it.

- Add in the salmon and toss it for another 1 minute.

- Add in the broccoli and toss it.

- Pour the rest of the marinade in the wok and sprinkle it with the sesame seeds.

Nutritional Information:

Calories: 217

Total Fat: 5g

Saturated Fat: 1g

Carbohydrates: 10g

Protein: 21g

Image sources/Printing information

Pictures cover: depositphotos.com;

@ ildi_papp; @ lateci; @ Shaiith79; @ Anna_Shepulova

Print edition black and white paperback:

Amazon Media EU S.à.r.l.

5 Rue Plaetis

L-2338 Luxembourg

Other printouts:

epubli, a service of neopubli GmbH, Berlin

Publisher:

BookRix GmbH & Co. KG

Sonnenstraße 23

80331 München

Deutschland

Printed in Great Britain
by Amazon